ANCHORED GRACE PUBLISHING

Glowing Strong Grandma

A 90-Day Large Print Devotional for Senior Women to Nourish Faith, Joy, and Strength

A Gift for You

Thank you for choosing this devotional.

To support your journey of faith, we created a special gift bundle for our readers.

Inside the Anchored Grace Reader Gift Bundle, you will receive:

A free digital devotional

Printable prayer journal pages

Scripture reflection cards

Bonus devotionals for different seasons of life

Daily encouragement from Anchored Grace

Simply scan the QR code below or visit the link to receive your free bundle.

devo.anchoredgraces.com/glowgrandmagift

Scan the QR code with your phone camera or type the link into your browser.

We pray these resources continue to encourage your heart each day.

Trusting God's Fresh Start

"Trust in the Lord with all your heart and lean not on your own understanding; in all your ways acknowledge Him, and He shall direct your paths."

Proverbs 3:5-6

DEVOTION

To embrace new beginnings is to trust that God has a beautiful plan for us, even when we feel lost or alone.

What new beginnings might God be inviting you to embrace in this season of your life? How can you trust Him more fully as you step into these opportunities?

_____
_____
_____
_____
_____

PRAYER

Dear Lord, thank You for the gift of new beginnings. Help me to trust in Your plan and to embrace the fresh starts You provide each day.

Every dawn is an invitation to rise anew, leaving yesterday behind and stepping boldly into God's grace.

"She opens her mouth with wisdom, and the teaching of kindness is on her tongue."

Proverbs 31:26

DEVOTION

Never underestimate the power of your words; they can be the very seeds of wisdom that nurture the next generation.

What life lesson do you cherish and wish to share with those you love most?

_____

_____

_____

_____

_____

PRAYER

Dear Lord, thank you for the wisdom you've granted us through our experiences. Help us to share our lessons with love and grace, guiding those we cherish on their journeys.

Sharing wisdom is like planting seeds; you never know when they will bloom.

Embracing Change in the New Year

"She is clothed with strength and dignity; she can laugh at the days to come."

Proverbs 31:25

DEVOTION

Change, like a new quilt, may seem daunting at first, but it often reveals a tapestry of unforeseen beauty and connection.

What changes do you feel God inviting you to embrace in this new year, and how can you open your heart to those opportunities?

_____

_____

_____

_____

_____

PRAYER

Dear God, as we step into this new year, grant us the courage to embrace change with grace. Help us recognize Your hand in every transition and trust that your plans are good. Amen.

Like the seasons that turn, we too can find beauty in the changes of life.

Praying for Our Families

"Do not be anxious about anything, but in every situation, by prayer and petition, with thanksgiving, present your requests to God."

Philippians 4:6-7

DEVOTION

We may not always be able to solve our family's problems, but we can faithfully lift them up to the Lord in prayer, trusting His perfect plan.

What are the specific needs and challenges your family faces that you can lift up in prayer today? How can you draw closer to God as you bring these concerns before Him?

_____

_____

_____

_____

_____

PRAYER

Dear Lord, thank You for the gift of family. Help me to cover them in prayer daily and trust in Your perfect will for their lives.

Great love is often expressed in quiet prayers.

The Blessing of Grandchildren

"Children's children are a crown to the aged, and parents are the pride of their children."

Proverbs 17:6

DEVOTION

The blessings of grandchildren remind us that life is filled with opportunities for connection, joy, and the endless sharing of love across generations.

What do you cherish most about the moments you've spent with your grandchildren?

_____

_____

_____

_____

_____

PRAYER

Dear Lord, thank You for the precious gift of grandchildren. May the time spent with them be filled with love and laughter, and may I always share Your wisdom and warmth with each cherished moment.

Grandchildren are not just a part of our legacy; they are the joy that colors our days.

Finding Joy in Simple Moments

"Rejoice in the Lord always. I will say it again: Rejoice!"

John 14:1-3

DEVOTION

In the tapestry of life, the most vibrant threads come from moments of connection and joy found in the ordinary.

What simple moment in your day brings you the most joy, and how can you cherish it more fully?

_____

_____

_____

_____

_____

PRAYER

Dear Lord, thank you for the gift of simple moments in our lives. Help us to recognize and embrace these joys, filling our hearts with gratitude.

Joy often hides in the small, ordinary moments we may overlook.

Renewing Body and Spirit

"Come to me, all you who are weary and burdened, and I will give you rest."

Matthew 11:28

DEVOTION

In our seasons of life, it's vital to carve out time for ourselves in the midst of our caring roles, for even the most devoted caregivers need moments of peace to rejuvenate.

What activities bring you a sense of peace and rest? How can you intentionally carve out time for these moments in your week?

_____

_____

_____

_____

_____

PRAYER

Dear Lord, thank You for the gift of rest. Help me to embrace the stillness of the Sabbath, renewing both my body and spirit in Your presence.

True rest is not merely the absence of activity, but the presence of peace.

One Week Together

You've just completed your first week of devotionals.

If these reflections have brought peace or encouragement into your day, would you consider sharing a short Amazon review?

devo.anchoredgraces.com/glowgrandma

Your words help other women discover devotionals that may support them on their own faith journey.

Thank you for spending these moments in reflection.

Passing Down Traditions

"Train up a child in the way he should go; even when he is old he will not depart from it."

Proverbs 22:6

DEVOTION

The sweetest gifts we can pass down to our grandchildren are the traditions and stories that make our families unique.

What traditions have you cherished and passed down to your family? How do these customs shape the bonds you share with them?

_____

_____

_____

_____

_____

PRAYER

Dear Lord, thank You for the beautiful traditions that weave our families together. Help us to honor and preserve these legacies, sharing love and wisdom with each generation.

Traditions are the threads that connect our past with our future.

The Power of Encouragement

"Anxiety weighs down the heart, but a kind word cheers it up.".

Proverbs 12:25

DEVOTION

Never underestimate the significance of a kind word; your encouragement can uplift a weary heart and change someone's day.

What words of encouragement have you shared with someone recently? How did it make you feel, and how did it impact their day?

_____

_____

_____

_____

_____

PRAYER

Dear Lord, thank you for the gift of encouragement. Help us to uplift those around us with kind words and heartfelt support, just as you uplift us.

Your words can be the sunshine for someone's cloudy day.

God's Faithfulness Through Generations

"For the Lord is good; His steadfast love endures forever, and His faithfulness to all generations."

Psalm 100:5

DEVOTION

Our stories of faith are gifts we can pass down, demonstrating how God's faithfulness sustains us and shapes our family legacy.

What stories of God's faithfulness have you seen unfold in your family over the years?

_ _

_ _

_ _

_ _

_ _

PRAYER

Dear Lord, thank You for Your unwavering faithfulness through all generations. Help us to continue sharing Your love and grace with our families, that they may also know Your presence in their lives.

Faithfulness is a gentle thread woven through the fabric of our family history.

Nurturing Friendships in Later Life

"Two are better than one, because they have a good reward for their toil; for if they fall, one will lift up his fellow."

Ecclesiastes 4:9-10

DEVOTION

Friendship is a beautiful tapestry, stitched together with love, laughter, and shared experiences, especially in these later years where we find strength in each other.

What does friendship mean to you in this season of your life?

_____

_____

_____

_____

_____

PRAYER

Dear Lord, help me cherish the friendships I have and seek new connections that bring joy and support. Grant me the wisdom to nurture these bonds with love and kindness.

Friendships are the heart's garden; they flourish with care and love.

Serving Others with a Grateful Heart

"Let each of you look not only to his own interests, but also to the interests of others."

Philippians 2:4

DEVOTION

The joy of serving others is magnified in our hearts when we approach it with gratitude, for it reminds us of the blessings we have to share.

What are the simple acts of kindness you can offer to those around you today, and how might you express your gratitude in those moments?

_____

_____

_____

_____

_____

PRAYER

Dear Lord, thank you for the gift of service and the joy it brings. Help me to see opportunities to lend a hand and share love with others, filled with a grateful heart.

Gratitude opens the door to a heart that serves.

The Comfort of God's Presence

"Where can I go from Your Spirit? Or where can I flee from Your presence? If I ascend to heaven, You are there; if I make my bed in hell, behold, You are there. If I take the wings of the morning and dwell in the uttermost parts of the sea, even there Your hand shall lead me, and Your right hand shall hold me."

John 14:1-3

DEVOTION

In the quiet moments of your life, remember that God's presence is always with you, a gentle reminder of love and comfort.

What moments in your daily life remind you of God's comforting presence? How can you seek that presence in times of uncertainty?

_____

_____

_____

_____

_____

PRAYER

Dear Lord, thank you for your unwavering presence in our lives. May we always feel your comforting touch and find peace in your love. Amen.

In the quiet moments of our days, God's presence whispers love and reassurance.

Embracing Grace
for Ourselves

"...after we have suffered a little while, God Himself will restore, confirm, strengthen, and establish us. He knows our hearts and our struggles, offering grace like a warm hug, reminding us that we're never alone."

1 Peter 5:10

DEVOTION

Embracing grace means allowing ourselves the freedom to begin again, knowing that our worth is not defined by our successes or failures.

What does it mean for you to truly embrace grace in your own life, allowing forgiveness and love to flow not just to others, but also to yourself?

_____

_____

_____

_____

_____

PRAYER

Dear Lord, thank You for the gift of grace that surrounds us each day. Help us to accept Your love and to share it with ourselves, so we can live fully in joy and peace.

Embracing grace means recognizing the beautiful worth in our imperfections.

Finding Purpose in Retirement

"Delight yourself in the LORD, and He will give you the desires of your heart."

Psalm 37:4

DEVOTION

In retirement, it's never too late to cultivate new passions and share your gifts with others.

What activities or passions have you set aside during your busy years that now spark excitement as you enter this new season of life?

————————————————————————

————————————————————————

————————————————————————

————————————————————————

————————————————————————

PRAYER

Dear Lord, thank you for the gift of this new chapter in my life. Help me to discover and embrace the purpose you have for me in my retirement, filling my days with joy and meaningful service.

Retirement is not the end of an era, but the beginning of an adventure.

God's Creation

"The grass withers, and the flowers fade, but the word of our God remains forever."

Isaiah 40:8

DEVOTION

Embrace the beauty of each season in life, knowing that even in winter, God's grace surrounds us, bringing warmth and joy.

What does the beauty of winter remind you about God's faithfulness in your life? How can you embrace this season of rest and reflection?

_____

_____

_____

_____

_____

PRAYER

Dear God, thank you for the beauty of winter and the quiet moments it brings. Help me to see your hand in every snowflake and to find joy in the stillness of this season.

In the quiet of winter, God whispers His love, inviting us to pause and reflect on the beauty around us.

Letting Go of Worry

"Therefore do not worry about tomorrow, for tomorrow will worry about itself. Each day has enough trouble of its own."

Matthew 6:34

DEVOTION

Letting go of worry opens the heart to experience the beauty of today, reminding us that God holds our futures with gentle hands.

What legacy do you hope to leave for your children and grandchildren as you pray for our nation in these times?

_____

_____

_____

_____

_____

PRAYER

Dear Lord, we lift our nation to You today. Please guide our leaders with wisdom and fill our hearts with peace, as we seek to support and uplift one another in Your love.

Prayer is the breath of our spirit; may we breathe deeply for our nation.

The Strength of a Praying Grandmother

"Therefore I tell you, whatever you ask in prayer, believe that you have received it, and it will be yours."

Mark 11:24

DEVOTION

Prayers offered in love can ignite hope and healing, bridging generational gaps with divine grace.

What has your prayer life looked like this week, and in what ways have you felt God's presence in your conversations with Him?

_____

_____

_____

_____

_____

PRAYER

Dear God, thank You for the gift of prayer and the loving hearts of grandmothers everywhere. Help us to trust in Your power as we lift our families to You each day.

Your prayers are a fabric woven with love, surrounding your family with warmth and strength.

Cherishing Family Memories

"Even to your old age and gray hairs I am he, I am he who will sustain you. I have made you and I will carry you; I will sustain you and I will rescue you."

Isaiah 46:4

DEVOTION

Our family stories, shared in love, are treasures that bind generations together.

What cherished family memory brings a smile to your face when you think about it?

‗‗‗‗‗‗‗‗‗‗‗‗‗‗‗‗‗‗‗‗‗‗‗‗‗

‗‗‗‗‗‗‗‗‗‗‗‗‗‗‗‗‗‗‗‗‗‗‗‗‗

‗‗‗‗‗‗‗‗‗‗‗‗‗‗‗‗‗‗‗‗‗‗‗‗‗

‗‗‗‗‗‗‗‗‗‗‗‗‗‗‗‗‗‗‗‗‗‗‗‗‗

‗‗‗‗‗‗‗‗‗‗‗‗‗‗‗‗‗‗‗‗‗‗‗‗‗

PRAYER

Dear Lord, thank You for the gift of family and the precious memories we create together. Help us to cherish each moment and pass down the love that binds us through the generations.

Memories are the threads that weave our families together.

God's Promises for the Future

"For I know the plans I have for you, declares the Lord, plans to prosper you and not to harm you, plans to give you hope and a future."

Jeremiah 29:11

DEVOTION

Even in times of uncertainty, God's promises remind us that we are never alone and that a beautiful future is being cultivated just for us.

What dreams or hopes do you hold for the future that you can entrust to God's loving care?

_____

_____

_____

_____

_____

PRAYER

Heavenly Father, thank You for the promises You have made for our future. Help me to lean into these truths and trust that You are guiding my path with love and wisdom.

Tomorrow holds the beauty of God's faithfulness, waiting to unfold in ways we cannot yet imagine.

The Joy of Giving

"The generous will themselves be blessed, for they share their food with the poor."

Proverbs 22:9

DEVOTION

In giving, we discover the true richness of our own hearts, filling them with joy and connection.

What special way can you share your love and resources with those around you today? How can your acts of kindness spark joy in both your heart and theirs?

_____

_____

_____

_____

_____

PRAYER

Dear Lord, thank You for the gift of giving. Help me find joy in sharing my blessings and spreading Your love to everyone I meet.

True joy is found not in what we have, but in what we share.

Three Weeks of Reflection

You've now spent several weeks walking through these devotionals.

If this book has encouraged your heart, a brief Amazon review helps other women find the same encouragement.

devo.anchoredgraces.com/glowgrandma

Your experience may guide someone else toward the hope they are searching for.

Thank you for being here.

Staying Connected with Loved Ones

"A friend loves at all times, and a brother is born for a time of adversity."

Proverbs 17:17

DEVOTION

Cherish and nurture your connections, for they are the cherished threads binding your heart to your loved ones.

What ways can you reach out to your loved ones this week, and how will you create moments of connection amidst your busy life?

———————————————————
———————————————————
———————————————————
———————————————————
———————————————————

PRAYER

Dear Lord, thank You for the gift of family and friends. Help me to cherish these connections and foster love in every moment we share. May I reach out with kindness and joy in my heart.

Love grows when nurtured, and every phone call or letter is a seed planted in the hearts of those we cherish.

The Blessing of Good Health

"Beloved, I pray that you may prosper in all things and be in health, just as your soul prospers."

3 John 1:2

DEVOTION

Our health is not just our physical strength, but also the energy we bring to our loved ones, allowing us to create beautiful memories together.

What does good health mean to you in this season of your life, and how do you see it as a blessing to share with your family?

_____

_____

_____

_____

_____

PRAYER

Dear Lord, thank You for the gift of health. May I cherish my well-being and use it to bring joy and love to those around me.

Health is not just the absence of illness; it's the presence of vitality to enjoy every moment.

Trusting God with Our Concerns

"Do not fear, for I am with you; do not be dismayed, for I am your God. I will strengthen you and help you; I will uphold you with my righteous right hand."

Isaiah 41:10

DEVOTION

Trusting God means releasing our concerns and believing He is weaving the threads of our family's stories with love and purpose.

What are the concerns that seem to weigh heavily on your heart today, and how can you bring them to God in trust?

_____

_____

_____

_____

_____

PRAYER

Dear Lord, as we gather our thoughts and worries, help us to lay them before You with unwavering trust. May Your peace wash over us, reminding us that we are never alone in our struggles.

Trusting God transforms our worries into whispers of hope.

The Gift of Laughter

"A joyful heart is good medicine, but a crushed spirit dries up the bones."

Proverbs 17:22

DEVOTION

Let laughter fill your heart and home; it is a reminder that joy can thrive even in the simplest moments.

What moments today have brought a smile to your face, and how can you share that laughter with others in your life?

_____

_____

_____

_____

_____

PRAYER

Dear Lord, thank You for the gift of laughter and the joy it brings. Help us to find humor in our days and share that warmth with those around us.

Laughter is a gentle reminder that joy can be found even in life's smallest moments.

Finding Peace in Uncertainty

"Peace I leave with you; my peace I give you. I do not give to you as the world gives. Do not let your hearts be troubled and do not be afraid."

John 14:27

DEVOTION

Trust that, like the flowers of the garden, your family will thrive in their own time, and let God's peace wash over you in moments of uncertainty.

What uncertainties are weighing on your heart today, and how can you invite peace into those moments?

PRAYER

Dear Lord, as I navigate these uncertain times, help me find comfort in Your presence. Fill my heart with peace and let my trust in You grow deeper each day.

Amid the storms of life, peace can bloom like a flower in the desert.

The Importance of Forgiveness

"Be kind to one another, tenderhearted, forgiving one another, as God in Christ forgave you."

Ephesians 4:32

DEVOTION

The grace of forgiveness can bring healing and connection, lighting the way for deeper family bonds in our golden years.

What memories or hurts from your past do you feel ready to release today in order to embrace a more peaceful heart?

_____

_____

_____

_____

_____

PRAYER

Dear Lord, help me to let go of the burdens I carry. Grant me the strength to forgive those who have hurt me, just as You forgive me every day. May Your love fill my heart and guide my actions.

Forgiveness is the gentle act of releasing ourselves from the chains of the past.

Celebrating Milestones

"Every good and perfect gift is from above, coming down from the Father of the heavenly lights, who does not change like shifting shadows."

James 1:17

DEVOTION

Every milestone, whether past or present, is an opportunity to honor cherished memories and embrace new beginnings, reminding us that love remains forever woven into our lives.

What milestones in your life have shaped who you are today, and how can you celebrate them with gratitude?

_____

_____

_____

_____

_____

PRAYER

Dear Lord, we thank You for the blessings of life and the many milestones that fill our years. Help us to cherish these moments and share our wisdom with those we love.

Every milestone is a thread in the beautiful tapestry of our lives.

Hope for the Year Ahead

"But those who hope in the Lord will renew their strength. They will soar on wings like eagles; they will run and not grow weary, they will walk and not be faint."

Isaiah 40:31

DEVOTION

In life, just as in gardening, the promise of hope lies in the ability to persevere and nurture what seems lost, trusting that new beginnings are always possible.

What hopes and dreams do you carry in your heart for the year ahead? How can you take even small steps toward them?

_____

_____

_____

_____

_____

PRAYER

Dear Lord, as I step into this new year, help me to embrace hope and joy in every moment. May my heart be open to your blessings and the potential that each day holds.

Hope lights the path ahead, reminding us that every new season brings fresh opportunities.

The Warmth of God's Love in Winter

"When you pass through the waters, I will be with you; and when you pass through the rivers, they will not sweep over you. When you walk through the fire, you will not be burned; the flames will not set you ablaze."

John 14:1-3

DEVOTION

In the coldest seasons of life, God's love is like a warm quilt, ready to wrap you up and keep you snug.

What are some ways you can recognize and embrace God's love in the chilly moments of winter?

_____

_____

_____

_____

_____

PRAYER

Dear Lord, thank You for the warmth of Your love that surrounds us, even in the coldest seasons. Help us to feel Your presence daily and to share that warmth with others. Amen.

In the stillness of winter, God's love is the gentle fire that burns within us.

The Power of a Gentle Word

"A gentle answer turns away wrath, but a harsh word stirs up anger."

Proverbs 15:1

DEVOTION

The most powerful gift we can offer our loved ones is not just our wisdom, but our gentle words that bring healing and support.

What gentle words have you spoken recently that may have lifted someone's spirit?

_____

_____

_____

_____

_____

PRAYER

Dear Lord, thank you for the power of our words. Help us to speak gently and wisely, sharing your love and encouragement with everyone we meet.

A gentle word can soften even the hardest heart.

Praying for Our Children's Marriages

"He who finds a wife finds what is good and receives favor from the Lord."

Proverbs 18:22

DEVOTION

As grandmothers, the love we pour into our prayers can become a gentle balm for our children's marriages, nurturing their relationships with the grace and wisdom we've gained over the years.

What specific qualities do you hope for in your children's marriages, and how can your prayers help nurture those desires?

———————————————
———————————————
———————————————
———————————————
———————————————

PRAYER

Dear Lord, please bless my children's marriages with love, patience, and understanding. Guide them through the challenges they may face and strengthen their bond each day.

Prayer is the bridge that connects our hopes for our children to God's heart for their marriages.

The Gift of Friendship

"I no longer call you servants, because a servant does not know his master's business. Instead, I have called you friends, for everything that I learned from my Father I have made known to you."

John 15:15

DEVOTION

True friendship, like a well-tended garden, brings beauty, joy, and support to our lives, reminding us that we are never alone.

What does friendship mean to you at this stage of your life, and how have your cherished connections shaped who you are today?

_____

_____

_____

_____

_____

PRAYER

Dear Lord, thank you for the precious gift of friendship. Help us nurture these bonds with love and laughter, and remind us of the joy that comes from sharing our lives with others.

Friendship is the thread that weaves our lives together, creating a tapestry rich in love and memories.

Finding Beauty in the Ordinary

"See, I am doing a new thing! Now it springs up; do you not perceive it? I am making a way in the wilderness and streams in the wasteland."

Isaiah 43:19

DEVOTION

Sometimes, all we need to do is pause and observe the world around us to find the beauty that is present in the ordinary.

What simple moments in your daily life bring you joy and remind you of the beauty that surrounds you?

—————————————————————————

—————————————————————————

—————————————————————————

—————————————————————————

—————————————————————————

PRAYER

Dear Lord, thank You for the everyday wonders that fill our lives with joy. Help me to open my eyes and heart to the beauty in the ordinary moments, letting them deepen my faith and gratitude.

Beauty often lies in the details we overlook—a soft breeze, the laughter of children, or a quiet cup of tea on a sunny afternoon.

Sharing Faith Stories with Grandchildren

"One generation commends your works to another; they tell of your mighty acts."

Psalm 145:4

DEVOTION

Every story shared is a thread woven into the fabric of our grandchildren's faith, teaching them that they are part of a God-written legacy.

What stories of faith do you cherish most, and how can you share them in a way that your grandchildren will understand and connect with?

_____

_____

_____

_____

_____

PRAYER

Dear Lord, may the stories of Your love and faithfulness flow from my heart to my grandchildren's ears. Help me to share with joy, wisdom, and grace as we connect through these precious moments.

Faith is a legacy, best shared through the warmth of our stories.

The Joy of Cooking for Family

"She rises while it is yet night and provides food for her household and portions for her maidens. She considers a field and buys it; with the fruit of her hands, she plants a vineyard."

Proverbs 31:15-16

DEVOTION

Cooking for family is not just about nourishing their bodies; it's about weaving together moments of love and connection that create lasting memories.

What is one special dish you can make for your family that brings back cherished memories for you?

_____

_____

_____

_____

_____

PRAYER

Dear Lord, thank you for the gift of family and the joy of cooking. May each meal we prepare be seasoned with love and sprinkled with laughter, nourishing not just our bodies but also our hearts.

Cooking is an act of love that brings generations together, creating bonds that last beyond the dinner table.

God's Love Never Fails

"So we have come to know and to believe the love that God has for us."

1 John 4:16

DEVOTION

Remember, dear ones, that no matter the trials you face, God's love never fails and always nourishes the roots of hope in your heart.

What moments in your life have you felt the unwavering presence of God's love, even amid challenges or uncertainty?

_____

_____

_____

_____

_____

PRAYER

Dear Lord, thank You for Your steadfast love that guides us each day. Help us to feel Your presence in our hearts and share that love generously with those around us. Amen.

Even in life's storms, God's love is our anchor, holding us firm and steady.

Acts of Kindness

"A generous person will prosper; whoever refreshes others will be refreshed."

Proverbs 11:25

DEVOTION

In kindness, we find the joy of connection, reminding us of the love that binds generations together.

What small act of kindness could you offer today that would bring a smile to someone's face or lighten their load?

_____

_____

_____

_____

_____

PRAYER

Dear Lord, thank You for the gift of kindness that flows from our hearts. Help us to be instruments of Your love, sharing small gestures that can make a big difference in the world. Amen.

Kindness is the language the deaf can hear and the blind can see.

Remembering Loved Ones

"...the righteous perish, and no one ponders it in his heart; devout men are taken away, and no one understands that the righteous are taken away to be spared from evil."

Isaiah 57:1-2

DEVOTION

Cherish the memories of your loved ones; they are forever a part of your heart's garden.

What cherished memories do you hold of the loved ones you have lost, and how do those memories shape who you are today?

_____

_____

_____

_____

_____

PRAYER

Dear Lord, thank you for the precious gift of our memories. May we find comfort in remembering our loved ones and joy in the legacy of love they left behind.

Even in their absence, the love we shared remains a guiding light in our hearts.

The Gift of a Loving Spouse

"For where your treasure is, there your heart will be also."

Matthew 6:21

DEVOTION

True love is a treasure that deepens with each passing year, reminding us to embrace every shared moment with gratitude.

What are some of the cherished moments you've shared with your spouse that make your heart smile?

_____

_____

_____

_____

_____

PRAYER

Dear Lord, thank You for the gift of love we share in our marriages. Help us to appreciate the small moments and to nurture that love each day.

Love is not just in the grand gestures, but in the quiet moments spent together.

Praying for Friendships

"I thank my God every time I remember you."

Philippians 1:3

DEVOTION

Your prayers for your grandchildren are powerful and can shape their lives in ways you may never fully see.

What qualities do you hope your grandchildren seek in their friendships?

_____

_____

_____

_____

_____

PRAYER

Dear Lord, I lift my grandchildren up to You, asking for Your guidance in their friendships. May they find companions who uplift and encourage them, and may Your love shine through them in all their interactions.

Friends are the mirrors reflecting our values; may they reflect kindness, loyalty, and warmth.

The Comfort of God's Word

"My comfort in my suffering is this: Your promise preserves my life."

Psalm 119:50

DEVOTION

In God's Word, we find the comfort that gently cradles our hearts through every season of life.

What verses from God's Word have brought you comfort in times of trouble?

_____
_____
_____
_____
_____

PRAYER

Dear Lord, I thank You for the gift of Your Word that guides and comforts me. Please help me to find peace in Your promises and to share that peace with those around me.

In every season of life, God's Word remains a steady anchor for our hearts.

The Joy of Family Gatherings

"Behold, children are a heritage from the LORD, the fruit of the womb a reward."

Psalm 127:3

DEVOTION

In every gathering, may we treasure the love and laughter that surrounds us, for these moments are God's sweetest gifts to our hearts.

What memories do you cherish most from family gatherings, and how do they fill your heart with joy today?

_____

_____

_____

_____

_____

PRAYER

Dear Lord, thank you for the gift of family and the joy that comes from gathering together. Help us to cherish these moments, filling our hearts with love and laughter. Amen.

Family gatherings are the threads that weave the fabric of our hearts.

The Blessing of Good Neighbors

"As iron sharpens iron, so one person sharpens another."

Proverbs 27:17

DEVOTION

Remember, dear ones, it is in nurturing our relationships with neighbors that we find true joy and support in life's journey.

What qualities do your neighbors possess that enrich your life, and how might you show appreciation for them today?

_____

_____

_____

_____

_____

PRAYER

Dear Lord, thank you for the neighbors you've placed in my life. Help me to cherish our connections and to share kindness with those living close by.

Good neighbors are like a cozy blanket, providing warmth and comfort in our daily lives.

Finding God in Quiet Moments

*"Be still,
and know that I am God."*

Psalm 46:10

DEVOTION

In every quiet moment, God whispers reassurance, inviting us to seek His presence amidst our busy lives.

What are some quiet moments in your day where you feel God's presence most closely?

_____

_____

_____

_____

_____

PRAYER

Dear Lord, thank you for the quiet moments when we can feel You near. May we find peace in these still times and let Your love fill our hearts.

In the stillness, God whispers His love and grace, inviting us to draw near.

Halfway Through Our Journey

You are now halfway through this devotional journey.

Many women discover this book through the thoughtful reviews shared by readers like you.

If these pages have supported your faith and daily reflection, would you consider sharing a short review on Amazon?

Your voice may help someone else find encouragement today.

devo.anchoredgraces.com/glowgrandma

The Importance of Listening

"If one gives an answer before he hears, it is his folly and shame."

Proverbs 18:13

DEVOTION

Take a moment to listen fully; it strengthens bonds and brings joy, not just to those who share their stories but to your heart as well.

What is one moment recently where you felt truly heard and how did it impact you?

PRAYER

Dear Lord, thank You for the gift of listening and for the ears You've given us to hear each other. Help us to engage deeply with those around us and reflect Your loving attentiveness in our conversations.

Listening is a sacred act; it allows us to touch the hearts of others.

The Blessing of a New Grandchild

"And when Esau looked up and saw the women and children, he said, 'Who are these with you?' Jacob said, 'The children God has graciously given your servant."

Genesis 33:5

DEVOTION

Every new grandchild is a precious gift, a special reminder that God's blessings continue to unfold in our lives, often in ways we least expect.

What joys and hopes do you hold in your heart as you welcome this new grandchild into your family?

_____

_____

_____

_____

_____

PRAYER

Dear Lord, thank You for the gift of this new grandchild. May Your love surround this precious child and may our hearts be filled with joy as we watch them grow.

New life brings renewed promise and a fresh perspective on love.

Trusting God with Our Hopes

"Yes, my soul, find rest in God; my hope comes from Him. Truly He is my rock and my salvation; He is my fortress, I will not be shaken."

Psalm 62:5-6

DEVOTION

As we release our dreams and desires into His hands, we open ourselves to the abundance of His grace and the joy of His unexpected blessings.

What hopes do you hold in your heart that you can trust God with today?

_____
_____
_____
_____
_____

PRAYER

Dear Lord, as I lay my hopes before You, help me to trust in Your perfect timing and wisdom. Fill my heart with peace and assurance as I lean into Your promises.

Trusting God transforms our hopes into a beautiful tapestry of His grace.

New Life in Christ

"...a garment of praise instead of a spirit of despair."

Isaiah 61:3

DEVOTION

Just as the earth awakens to new life each spring, may we also open our hearts to the renewal that Christ offers, trusting in His promise to bring beauty from our struggles.

What new beginnings is God inviting you to embrace this spring, and how can you nurture that new life in your heart?

PRAYER

Dear Lord, thank You for the gift of new life in Christ. Help me to open my heart to the beauty of spring, embracing the fresh starts You offer every day. Amen.

In Christ, every spring carries the promise of renewal and hope.

The Joy of Gardening

"And why do you worry about clothes? See how the lilies of the field grow. They do not labor or spin. Yet I tell you that not even Solomon in all his splendor was dressed like one of these."

Matthew 6:28-30

DEVOTION

Even in seasons of grief, there is joy to be discovered in nurturing life and embracing the beauty that surrounds us

What brings you joy in your garden today, and how does it mirror the growth you see in your life and loved ones?

————————————————————
————————————————————
————————————————————
————————————————————
————————————————————

PRAYER

Dear Lord, thank You for the beauty of creation that surrounds us. Help us to find peace and joy in every seed we plant and every bloom we see. May our gardens be a reflection of Your love and grace.

Just as each plant has its season, so do we; every stage of life carries its own beauty and purpose.

Praying for Our Church Family

"Therefore encourage one another and build each other up, just as in fact you are doing."

1 Thessalonians 5:11

DEVOTION

In praying for our church family, we discover that in helping others, we often find healing for ourselves, too.

What faces come to mind when you think of your church family? How can you lift them up in prayer today?

PRAYER

Dear Lord, thank You for the blessing of our church family. Help us to support and love one another in prayer, just as You care for each of us.

Prayer is the thread that binds our hearts together.

The Blessing of a Daughter

"She opens her mouth with wisdom, and the teaching of kindness is on her tongue."

Proverbs 31:26

DEVOTION

The legacy of love lives on in our daughters, reminding us that even in loss, we carry forward a piece of our hearts through them.

What are the unique ways your daughter has blessed your life, and how can you express your gratitude for her presence today?

_____

_____

_____

_____

_____

PRAYER

Dear Lord, thank You for the gift of our daughters. Help us to cherish the bond we share and to lift them up in love and grace every day.

Daughters are not just a part of our lives; they are the heartbeats of our souls.

The Gift of a Son

"When they saw the star, they rejoiced with exceeding great joy. And when they had come into the house, they saw the young Child with Mary His mother, and fell down and worshiped Him. And when they had opened their treasures, they presented gifts to Him: gold, frankincense, and myrrh."

Matthew 2:10-11

DEVOTION

The love of a son, no matter the circumstances, is a profound reminder of joy and connection that can carry us through the hardest times.

*What memories do you cherish most
about your son, and how have they
shaped your journey as a mother
and now a grandmother?*

_____

_____

_____

_____

_____

PRAYER

Dear God, thank you for the
beautiful gift of a son, for the
laughter and love he has brought
into our lives. May I always
treasure our moments together
and find joy in his growth.

A son is a wonderful reminder that
love can only multiply.

The Importance of Patience

"Let perseverance finish its work so that you may be mature and complete, not lacking anything."

James 1:4

DEVOTION

In our journey, patience teaches us that beautiful fruits emerge in their own time, bringing rewards we often cannot see at first.

What does patience look like in your daily life, and how can you cultivate it in your relationships with family and friends?

_____

_____

_____

_____

_____

PRAYER

Dear Lord, thank You for the gift of time and for the lessons it brings. Help me to embrace each moment with grace and patience as I navigate the blessings and challenges of life.

Patience is the gentle strength that allows love to blossom in its own time.

The Power of a Thankful Heart

"In everything give thanks; for this is the will of God in Christ Jesus concerning you."

1 Thessalonians 5:18

DEVOTION

Through the simple act of thankfulness, we can transform life's little challenges into opportunities for joy and love.

What are three things you can be thankful for today, and how have they impacted your heart and spirit?

_____

_____

_____

_____

_____

PRAYER

Dear God, thank you for the gift of each new day. Help me to see the blessings in my life and cultivate a heart overflowing with gratitude.

A thankful heart transforms ordinary days into extraordinary blessings.

Celebrating Women

"But I will hope continually and will praise you yet more and more."

Psalm 71:14

DEVOTION

In every friendship and support we offer one another, we create a tapestry of love that celebrates our shared journey.

What women have inspired you in your life, and how can you honor their contributions in your own journey today?

_____

_____

_____

_____

_____

PRAYER

Dear God, thank You for the incredible women who have paved the way for us. Help us to celebrate their strength and wisdom as we reflect on their impact in our lives and communities.

Every woman is a story, a legacy of strength, resilience, and love.

The Blessing
of a Close Friend

"Therefore encourage one another and build each other up, just as in fact you are doing."

1 Thessalonians 5:11

DEVOTION

The blessing of a close friend reminds us that love and encouragement can brighten even the cloudiest of days.

What does your close friend mean to you, and how have they enriched your life through shared experiences and heartfelt conversations?

_____

_____

_____

_____

_____

PRAYER

Dear Lord, thank you for the precious gift of friendship. Please nurture and strengthen the bonds we share, reminding us daily of the love and joy that true friends bring.

Friendship is a treasure that shines brightest in life's gentle moments and steadfast storms.

The Gift of Music

"Make a joyful noise to the Lord, all the earth! Serve the Lord with gladness; come into his presence with singing!"

Psalm 100:1-2

DEVOTION

Even in loss, music can be a powerful reminder of love, helping us navigate our grief while keeping cherished memories alive.

What songs bring back cherished memories for you?

PRAYER

Dear Lord, thank You for the gift of music that enriches our souls. Help us to find joy and peace in the melodies that surround us, and may we use them to uplift ourselves and those we love.

Music is the language of the heart, speaking what words cannot express.

Praying for Our Community

"Therefore I tell you, whatever you ask in prayer, believe that you have received it, and it will be yours."

Mark 11:24

DEVOTION

No matter the pain of loss, reaching out through prayer can bring healing to our hearts and strengthen the bonds within our community.

What are some specific needs in your community that you can bring before God in prayer today?

_____

_____

_____

_____

_____

PRAYER

Dear Lord, we lift up our community to You, asking for wisdom, compassion, and unity among our neighbors. Help us to be instruments of Your peace and love as we pray and support one another.

Together in prayer, we become the heartbeat of our community.

The Joy of Spring Cleaning

"*Create in me a clean heart, O God, and renew a right spirit within me.*"

Psalm 51:10

DEVOTION

Just as we clear the clutter from our homes, let us also make space in our hearts for new blessings and fresh experiences.

What hidden treasures or memories do you uncover when you take the time to tidy up your space?

PRAYER

Dear Lord, thank you for the gift of a new season and the opportunity for renewal. As we clear away the clutter in our homes, help us to also embrace the changes in our hearts. May your joy fill our spirits as we refresh our surroundings.

Just as the flowers bloom with the season, so too can our hearts blossom with joy through the act of letting go.

The Beauty of God's Creation

"O Lord, how manifold are Your works! In wisdom, You have made them all; the earth is full of Your creatures. There is the sea, vast and spacious, teeming with creatures beyond number—living things both large and small."

Psalm 104:24-25

DEVOTION

Every day holds the opportunity to witness the beauty of God's creation; let it inspire your heart and remind you of His infinite love.

What special moment in nature have you recently experienced that reminded you of God's loving presence?

_____

_____

_____

_____

_____

PRAYER

Dear Lord, thank you for the beauty that surrounds us each day. Help us to see and appreciate your creation in all its forms, from the smallest flower to the vast sky above. Amen.

In the gentle whisper of the breeze, we hear the heart of our Creator.

The Importance of Rest

"He makes me lie down in green pastures. He leads me beside still waters."

Psalm 23:2

DEVOTION

Sometimes, a little pause in our busy lives can refresh both our spirits and our hearts, reminding us that rest is a vital part of our journey.

What does rest mean to you in this season of life, and how might you embrace it more intentionally in your daily routine?

_____

_____

_____

_____

_____

PRAYER

Dear Lord, thank You for the gift of rest and quiet moments. Help me to prioritize my need for peace and refreshment, so I may embrace each day with joy and strength. Amen.

Rest is not a luxury; it is a meeting place with our Creator.

The Blessing of a Grandson

"...impress God's teachings on our children, sharing His love and wisdom across generations."

Deuteronomy 6:7

DEVOTION

Cherish each moment with your grandson, for in his innocence, there lies a profound connection to your legacy of love and faith.

What are the special moments you cherish with your grandson that remind you of the joy he brings into your life? How can you nurture those moments even more?

PRAYER

Dear Lord, thank You for the gift of my grandson. May our bond grow stronger and may I always see the beauty in our shared moments.

Each laugh, each hug, and each story shared are treasures woven into the fabric of our hearts.

The Gift of a Granddaughter

"Only be careful, and watch yourselves closely so that you do not forget the things your eyes have seen or let them fade from your heart as long as you live. Teach them to your children and to their children after them."

Deuteronomy 4:9

DEVOTION

Every moment spent with your granddaughter is a precious treasure that not only enriches her life but also deepens your legacy and joy.

What special moments have you shared with your granddaughter that fill your heart with joy?

_____

_____

_____

_____

_____

PRAYER

Dear God, thank you for the precious gift of granddaughters. May our bonds deepen and our shared memories grow sweeter with each passing day.

Every moment spent with a granddaughter is a treasure, a thread woven into the fabric of your heart.

Celebrating
Family Roots

"A good man leaves an inheritance to his children's children."

Proverbs 13:22

DEVOTION

The greatest gift we can give our grandchildren is the legacy of our stories and the values that have shaped our lives.

What are the cherished stories and traditions from your family that you can share with your grandchildren today?

_____

_____

_____

_____

_____

PRAYER

Dear Lord, thank You for the gift of family and the rich tapestry of our heritage. May we honor and celebrate our roots, sharing love and wisdom with those who come after us.

Roots nourish us, and the stories we pass down are the branches that keep our family tree flourishing.

The Power of Prayer

"And whatever you ask in prayer, you will receive, if you have faith."

Matthew 21:22

DEVOTION

Remember, every prayer, no matter how small, carries the strength of love and intention, forging a bond between you and your loved ones that nothing can break.

What moments in your life have shown you the importance of turning to prayer? How has prayer shaped your relationship with God and those around you?

_____

_____

_____

_____

_____

PRAYER

Dear Lord, thank you for the gift of prayer. Help me to remember that in every moment, whether joyful or challenging, I can always turn to you for guidance and comfort.

Prayer is the bridge that connects our hearts to the Father's presence.

"I will open rivers on the bare heights, and fountains in the midst of the valleys; I will make the wilderness a pool of water, and the dry land springs of water."

Isaiah 41:18

DEVOTION

Sometimes, renewal comes from nurturing old dreams while embracing new possibilities.

*What does renewal mean to you,
and how can you embrace this
season of spring in your own life?*

_____

_____

_____

_____

_____

PRAYER

Dear Lord, thank you for the
beauty of spring and the promise of
renewal it brings. May we open our
hearts to new beginnings and be
filled with your love and hope as
we step into this season.

Just as flowers bloom after the frost,
our hearts can also blossom in times
of change.

The Blessing of Family Traditions

"And these words that I command you today shall be on your heart. You shall teach them diligently to your children and shall talk of them when you sit in your house, and when you walk by the way, and when you lie down, and when you rise."

Deuteronomy 6:6-7

DEVOTION

Grandchildren may forget the specifics of our stories, but they will always remember the warmth of our traditions and the love that surrounded them.

What family traditions bring you the most joy and connection? How do they reflect your love for your family and your hopes for future generations?

_____

_____

_____

_____

_____

PRAYER

Dear Lord, thank You for the gift of family and the traditions that bind us together. Help us to cherish these moments and pass down our love and wisdom to those who come after us.

Traditions are the threads that weave the fabric of our family stories.

The Joy of Learning New Things

"The righteous will flourish like a palm tree, they will grow like a cedar of Lebanon; planted in the house of the Lord, they will flourish in the courts of our God. They will still bear fruit in old age, they will stay fresh and green."
Psalm 92:12-14

DEVOTION

Life is a beautiful journey of continuous learning, and embracing new experiences can bring fresh joy and connection, no matter your age.

What new skill or hobby have you been curious about lately, and how might exploring it bring you joy and connection with others?

PRAYER

Dear Lord, thank You for the gift of curiosity and the joy that comes with learning. Help me to embrace new opportunities with an open heart and a willing spirit.

Learning is a lifelong journey, and each new experience can weave beautiful threads into the tapestry of our lives.

The Gift
of Hospitality

"Share with the Lord's people who are in need. Practice hospitality."

Romans 12:13

DEVOTION

A warm invitation can turn a stranger into a friend and make the simplest moments unforgettable.

What memories do you cherish of gathering friends and family around your table?

_____

_____

_____

_____

_____

PRAYER

Dear Lord, thank you for the gift of community and the warmth of shared meals. Help me to open my home and my heart to others, creating a space filled with love and joy.

Hospitality is not just about food; it's about making others feel at home in your heart.

A Moment of Gratitude

If this devotional has brought moments of peace, strength, or reflection into your life, a short review on Amazon can help others discover it too.

devo.anchoredgraces.com/glowgrandma

Even a few words about your experience can make a meaningful difference.

Thank you for continuing this journey.

The Blessing of a Loving Heart

"We love because he first loved us."

1 John 4:19

DEVOTION

When we open our hearts to love freely, we create a cherished legacy that continues to bless generations.

What does it mean to you to have a loving heart, and how can you express that love in your daily interactions with family and friends?

_____

_____

_____

_____

_____

PRAYER

Dear God, thank you for the gift of love in our hearts. Help us to share that love freely, nurturing those around us with kindness and compassion.

A loving heart not only transforms the lives of others but enriches our own journey.

The Importance of Faithfulness

"Therefore, my dear brothers and sisters, stand firm. Let nothing move you. Always give yourselves fully to the work of the Lord, because you know that your labor in the Lord is not in vain."

1 Corinthians 15:58

DEVOTION

Faithfulness, like a well-tended garden, requires patience and dedication, but the beauty it brings will bless not only you but generations to come.

What does *faithfulness mean to you, and how has it shaped your relationships and experiences over the years?*

_____

_____

_____

_____

_____

PRAYER

Dear Lord, thank You for the gift of faithfulness in our lives. Help us to embrace and embody this quality, nurturing the bonds we have with family, friends, and You.

Faithfulness is the quiet strength that binds hearts together and nurtures a legacy of love.

The Gift of a Loving Pet

"Your righteousness is like the mighty mountains, your justice like the great deep. You, Lord, preserve both people and animals."

Psalm 36:6

DEVOTION

Cherish the simple joys that a loving pet brings into your life, as their unwavering companionship reflects the love of God in our everyday moments.

What joy does your furry friend bring to your life, and how have they taught you about love and companionship?

_____

_____

_____

_____

_____

PRAYER

Dear Lord, thank You for the gift of our beloved pets. May we always cherish the unconditional love they bring into our lives. Help us to reflect Your love through the care we give them.

The heart grows warmer with every wag of a tail and every gentle purr.

The Joy of Sharing Stories

"But as for you, speak the things which are proper for sound doctrine."

Titus 2:1

DEVOTION

Every story you share holds the power to connect generations, bridging the past and the present with love and laughter.

What story has most shaped your life, and how can sharing it bring joy to others today?

PRAYER

Dear Lord, thank You for the gift of memories and the stories that bind us together. Help me to share my experiences with love and wisdom, bringing joy and lessons to those who listen.

Every story shared is a bridge built between generations.

The Blessing of a Strong Marriage

"A wife of noble character who can find? She is worth far more than rubies. Her husband has full confidence in her and lacks nothing of value."

Proverbs 31:10-11

DEVOTION

A strong marriage is a beautiful example of enduring love that nourishes not only the couple but also the generations that follow.

What are some of the ways your strong marriage has shaped your life and the lives of those around you?

_____

_____

_____

_____

_____

PRAYER

Dear Lord, thank you for the gift of love that we share in our marriages. Help us to appreciate and nurture these bonds daily and to carry that love into the lives of our families.

Love is a lifelong journey – the roots that nourish our family tree.

The Power of Hope

"May the God of hope fill you with all joy and peace as you trust in Him."

Romans 15:13

DEVOTION

Hope clings to the heart and can transform even the most somber days into a tapestry of love and connection.

What brings you hope in your daily life, and how can you nurture that hope in times of difficulty?

_____

_____

_____

_____

_____

PRAYER

Dear God, thank You for the gift of hope that anchors our souls. May we feel Your presence in our hearts and find comfort in the promises You have for us each day. Amen.

Hope lights the path even in the darkest moments, guiding us toward the beauty of tomorrow.

Preparing for Easter

"He is not here; for He has risen, as He said. Come, see the place where He lay."

Matthew 28:6

DEVOTION

Let us embrace this Easter season as a beautiful opportunity to share our faith, cherishing both the simplest joys and the profound truths with those we love.

What does Easter mean to you personally, and how can you prepare your heart and home to embrace its joy this year?

_____

_____

_____

_____

_____

PRAYER

Dear Lord, as Easter approaches, help us to reflect on your love and grace. Fill our hearts with joy and anticipation for the celebration of new life through your resurrection.

Preparing for Easter is like nurturing a garden; the more care and love we invest, the more beautiful the blooms we will see.

Welcoming Jesus

"The crowds that went ahead of him and those that followed shouted, 'Hosanna to the Son of David!' 'Blessed is he who comes in the name of the Lord!' 'Hosanna in the highest heaven!"

Matthew 21:9

DEVOTION

We learn that welcoming others, much like welcoming Jesus into our hearts, creates bonds of love and joy that fill our lives with meaning.

What does it mean for you to welcome Jesus into your everyday life this Palm Sunday?

_____

_____

_____

_____

_____

PRAYER

Dear Lord, thank You for the gift of Your Son and the joy He brings into our lives. Help us to open our hearts wide and embrace Him as we prepare for this special day.

Welcoming Jesus is not just a gesture; it's a heartfelt invitation to let Him walk alongside us in our journey.

He Is Risen!

"I am the resurrection and the life. He who believes in me will live, even though he dies; and whoever lives and believes in me will never die."

John 11:25-26

DEVOTION

This Easter, let the hope of resurrection fill your heart with joy, reminding you that love is everlasting.

What does the resurrection of Jesus mean for you in this season of your life, and how can you share that hope with those around you?

_____

_____

_____

_____

_____

PRAYER

Dear Lord, thank You for the gift of Your Son and the joy of His resurrection. Help us to carry this hope in our hearts today, sharing it with family and friends in meaningful ways.

He is risen not just to offer us eternal life but to fill our days with purpose and joy.

Caring for God's Creation

"You will go out in joy and be led forth in peace; the mountains and hills will burst into song before you, and all the trees of the field will clap their hands."

Isaiah 55:12

DEVOTION

Every small act of caring for the earth brings us closer to God and to the beauty of community, building a legacy of stewardship for the generations to come.

What do you cherish most about the beauty of nature, and how can you share that love with your family and community?

PRAYER

Dear Creator, thank you for the gift of your creation that surrounds us every day. Help us to cherish and protect the earth, nurturing it for future generations to enjoy. Amen.

Every flower, every tree, is a reminder of God's boundless love and artistry.

Praying for Generations to Come

"Let your roots grow down into Him, and let your lives be built on Him. Then your faith will grow strong in the truth you were taught, and you will overflow with thankfulness."

Colossians 2:7

DEVOTION

Our prayers today can build a legacy of faith for the generations yet to come.

What dreams do you hold in your heart for the generations that will come after you? How can your prayers today shape their paths tomorrow?

_____

_____

_____

_____

_____

PRAYER

Dear Lord, thank you for the gift of family and the legacy of faith. May my prayers cover my loved ones and their future, guiding them closer to You each day.

Your whispers of love today can echo in the hearts of those yet to be born.

Embracing Change with Grace

"Forget the former things; do not dwell on the past. See, I am doing a new thing! Now it springs up; do you not perceive it? I am making a way in the wilderness and streams in the wasteland."

Isaiah 43:18-19

DEVOTION

Embracing change allows us to recognize the beauty in new beginnings and the bonds that grow stronger through life's transitions.

What changes have you faced recently, and how can you open your heart to embrace them with grace and gratitude?

_____

_____

_____

_____

_____

PRAYER

Dear God, thank you for the gift of each new day. Help me to see the beauty in change and to trust in your plans for my life.

Embracing change is not about losing what we love; it's about finding new ways to love what remains.

Creating
New Traditions

"This is my commandment, that you love one another as I have loved you."

John 15:12

DEVOTION

Traditions don't just carry the past; they also create beautiful moments in the present.

What new traditions could you create with your grandchildren that would bring joy and strengthen your bond?

_____

_____

_____

_____

_____

PRAYER

Dear God, thank you for the gift of family. Please help me to create special moments with my grandchildren that will last a lifetime. Amen.

Traditions weave the fabric of our family's love.

Passing Down
Secret Family Recipes

"Stand up in the presence of the elderly, and show respect for the aged."

Leviticus 19:32

DEVOTION

Our family recipes are not just about nourishment; they are a legacy of love and tradition that we pass on with every meal shared.

What cherished recipes have been passed down in your family, and how do they connect you to your loved ones?

_____

_____

_____

_____

_____

PRAYER

Dear God, thank you for the gift of family and the love expressed through our recipes. May our kitchens be filled with laughter and the warmth of shared memories as we pass down our traditions.

Every recipe tells a story; each dish is a thread that weaves our family tapestry together.

The Gift of Togetherness

"A joyful heart makes a cheerful face, but by sorrow of heart, the spirit is crushed."

Proverbs 15:13

DEVOTION

Every moment spent in laughter and play with our loved ones builds cherished memories that last a lifetime.

What activities bring you joy and laughter with your loved ones? How can you cultivate more moments of shared joy in your life?

_____

_____

_____

_____

_____

PRAYER

Dear Lord, thank you for the gift of family and the joy of laughter. Help us to create and cherish moments of play and togetherness with those we love.

Laughter is the sun that drives winter from the human face.

Near the End of Our Journey

You have spent many days reflecting through these devotionals.

If this book has supported your spiritual journey, sharing a short review on Amazon helps more women discover these pages of encouragement.

devo.anchoredgraces.com/glowgrandma

Your story may be the reason another woman finds hope.

Speaking
Words of Blessing

"The tongue has the power of life and death, and those who love it will eat its fruit."

Proverbs 18:21

DEVOTION

Speak words of blessing over your loved ones daily, for your encouragement can plant seeds of love that flourish through seasons of life.

What words of blessing can you speak over your loved ones today to uplift their spirits and encourage their hearts?

_____

_____

_____

_____

_____

PRAYER

Dear God, thank you for the gift of family. Help us to recognize the power of our words, and may they always reflect Your love and grace as we speak blessings over those we cherish.

Your words have the power to shape the world around you; let them be filled with love and kindness.

Finding Beauty in Autumn's Changes

"And why do you worry about clothes? See how the flowers of the field grow. They do not labor or spin. Yet I tell you that not even Solomon in all his splendor was dressed like one of these."

Matthew 6:28-29

DEVOTION

As you embrace the richness of this season, remember that change is not to be feared but celebrated, for it often leads us to a more beautiful path ahead.

What changes in your life have brought you unexpected beauty this autumn? Can you see the blessings in the transition around you?

_____

_____

_____

_____

_____

PRAYER

Dear God, thank you for the beauty of this season and the wisdom that comes with change. Help us embrace the transformations in our lives, trusting that each one brings us closer to Your love and grace.

Autumn teaches us that change can be beautiful, and sometimes the most colorful lessons come from letting go.

Sharing Stories Around the Table

"And they shall be as a tree planted by the rivers of water, that bringeth forth his fruit in his season."

Psalm 1:3

DEVOTION

Every story you share is like a seed planted in the hearts of your loved ones, growing into understanding and wisdom.

What stories from your own life do you cherish the most?

PRAYER

Dear Lord, thank You for the gift of family and the wisdom of shared stories. May our conversations around the table be filled with love, laughter, and the richness of our experiences.

Every story shared is a thread woven into the fabric of our family, connecting us across generations.

Savoring God's Creation Outdoors

"For since the creation of the world God's invisible qualities— his eternal power and divine nature—have been clearly seen, being understood from what has been made, so that people are without excuse."

Romans 1:20

DEVOTION

Every time we step outside, we have an opportunity to connect with God through His wondrous creation, finding beauty in the details and peace for our hearts.

What does the beauty of a flower or the song of a bird reveal to you about God's love for creation and for you?

————————————————————————

————————————————————————

————————————————————————

————————————————————————

————————————————————————

PRAYER

Dear Lord, thank You for the gift of nature and for the moments spent in Your beautiful creation. Help us to slow down and truly savor the wonders You have placed around us.

To walk among the flowers is to walk in the presence of the Creator.

Walking in God's Presence

"You make known to me the path of life; in your presence there is fullness of joy; at your right hand are pleasures forevermore."

Psalm 16:11

DEVOTION

We can find God in the simple moments of our days, reminding us that His presence brings joy and peace.

What does it mean for you to consciously walk in God's presence each day, and how can you cultivate this awareness in your life?

_____

_____

_____

_____

_____

PRAYER

Dear Heavenly Father, thank You for the gift of Your constant presence. Help us to feel Your love surrounding us in every moment and guide us to share that love with those around us.

Walking in God's presence turns ordinary moments into sacred encounters.

More Devotionals
from Anchored Grace

If this devotional encouraged your heart, you may also enjoy these devotionals from Anchored Grace.

- 365 Day Devotional for Women
- 90 Day Devotional for Women Seeking Peace
- 90 Day Devotional for Women Facing Anxiety and Stress
- 90 Day Devotional for Women 50+
- Guided Prayer Journal for Women

Search **"Anchored Grace Devotional"** on Amazon to discover more devotionals designed to support your journey of faith.

Thank You
for Walking This Journey

Thank you for spending this devotional journey with Anchored Grace.

If this devotional encouraged your heart, strengthened your faith, or brought peace to your daily routine, would you consider leaving a short review on Amazon?

devo.anchoredgraces.com/glowgrandma

Reviews help other women discover devotionals that may support them through their own seasons of life.

Even a single sentence about your experience can make a difference.

We are grateful you chose Anchored Grace.